GIN THE MOOD

MOOD

50 GIN COCKTAIL RECIPES THAT ARE JUST THE TICKET

DOG 'n' BONE

Published in 2019 by Dog 'n' Bone Books
An imprint of Ryland Peters & Small Ltd
20–21 Jockey's Fields
London WC1R 4BW

341 E 116th St
New York, NY 10029

www.rylandpeters.com

10 9 8 7 6

Text © Michael Butt, Adam Elmegirab, Ben Reed,
William Yeoward 2019

Design, photography, and illustrations © Dog 'n' Bone Books 2019

A CIP catalog record for this book is available from
the Library of Congress and the British Library.

ISBN: 978 1 912983 02 5

Printed in China

Designer: Eoghan O'Brien
Recipe credits: see page 64
Photography credits: see page 64
Illustrator: Blaire Frame

CONTENTS

INTRODUCTION

While vodka might espouse the joys of unusual filtration processes, and whiskey prattles on about single malt Scotch or rare expressions of aged bourbon, gin instead sits back and lets its impressive cocktail CV do the talking. This venerable spirit was there at the conception of countless classic cocktails—the archetypal Martinez, the legendary Martini, and the peerless Negroni—and continues to be found front and center at the bar today, forming the backbone of many award-winning contemporary creations.

Versatile, adroit, and capable of giving any drink the satisfying spike of alcohol it needs, the following 50 recipes celebrate gin, the spirit that will always be the discerning bartender's go-to choice for crafting a perfectly balanced cocktail. Are you sitting comfortably? Then we'll drink gin.

SIMPLE SYRUP

Before we start, here's a recipe for Simple Syrup, which is a key ingredient in a whole host of the recipes featured in the book.

Mix superfine (caster) sugar and water in equal quantities by weight and stir. The mixture will be cloudy at first, but keep stirring and eventually it will form a clear syrup. This will keep in the fridge for 3 weeks.

INGREDIENTS

Superfine (caster) sugar

Water

DRY MARTINI

Although the world's most popular cocktail is the Margarita, the most recognized image for a cocktail is the Dry Martini, presented in a V-shaped cocktail glass. Few drinks allow the elegant consumption of virtually neat alcohol, and the huge number of variations inherent in the recipe allow for that most precious of commodities in our identikit world: personalization. A favorite gin (almost any will make a good Martini), a particular vermouth, the ratio of these ingredients (gin heavy for a dry Martini, 2 parts gin to one vermouth for a "wetter" drink, and choice of garnish mean it's easy to make the Martini your own.

Martinis must be COLD! Each aspect of the method must be designed to produce the coldest drink possible, with the ideal serving temperature 19°F (-7°C). To achieve this, it is vital to keep the glass in the freezer until the last moment, making sure the garnish is ready and the drinker keen in anticipation.

Stir the chosen amounts of gin and vermouth together with cubed ice. Avoid using frozen gin because very little water is added from melting ice, and the drink will be too strong— to achieve the standard optimum of 28% ABV, a good amount of water needs to be added. If you have a steel-walled (not glass) vacuum flask, stirring the drink inside will maximize the chilling effect of the ice and allow for

dilution—a digital thermometer is useful to check that the correct temperature is reached.

Strain the drink into a frozen coupe or Martini glass and garnish with citrus peel or olives, but remember that a warm garnish will undo all your good work in making a cold drink, so keep them in the refrigerator before adding or serve them on the side.

MARTINEZ

The union of spirit, vermouth, and bitters has long been celebrated in the world of mixed drinks, going back to the late 19th century when the Martinez first surfaced. The premise is relatively simple: take a spirit, balance it with a ratio of vermouth, and then finish it with bitters. In the past, bartenders would add further accents with dashes of syrups and liqueurs such as absinthe, curaçao, maraschino, and amari. A modern Martinez is often served

with a ratio of two parts spirit to one part vermouth, but this version is an older-style serve: two parts of vermouth to one of spirit. This provides a more flavorful beverage that is more "sessionable." Be sure to use an Old Tom gin with an ABV of around 45% so that it doesn't get lost in the drink.

Add all the ingredients to a cocktail shaker, fill it with cubed ice, and briskly stir for around 15–20 seconds. Strain into a pre-chilled coupe or Martini glass and garnish.

SMOKY MARTINI

GLASSWARE
Coupe or Martini glass

GARNISH
Olive

INGREDIENTS
2 parts (2 oz./ 50 ml) gin

1 dash dry vermouth

1 dash smoky whisky

Here's an interesting tweak to a Martini. Adding a dash of smoky whisky in place of vermouth makes the cocktail an altogether different beast. A peaty Scotch from Islay would work particularly well here, such as those from Laphroaig or Lagavulin.

Add the ingredients to a shaker filled with cracked ice. Shake sharply and strain into a frosted coupe or Martini glass with a lemon-zested rim. Garnish with an olive.

HANKY PANKY

Coupe or Martini glass

Orange twist

1/3 part Fernet Branca

2 parts Punt e Mes vermouth

2 parts Bombay Sapphire gin

Fernet Branca is supposed to have excellent digestive qualities and many Italians who subscribe to this happy belief. The fact that the Hanky Panky cocktail was created in 1904 by Ada Coleman, who was the first-ever female bartender at London's famous cocktail haunt the Savoy Hotel, gives it added charisma.

Pre-chill a glass. Stir all the ingredients over ice in a mixing jug (the cocktail should not be shaken, as this would "bruise" the gin); strain the mixture into the glass from high above, in order to aerate it. Mist the orange twist over the cocktail, then gently drop it into the glass.

GIMLET

GLASSWARE

Coupe or Martini
glass

GARNISH

1 lime wedge
or twist

Sharp yet sweet, the Gimlet is an excellent choice when the summer months come around. The cocktail's original recipes were made with equal parts gin to lime cordial, but to the modern palate this can be a little cloying. As a result, most Gimlets served today come with a higher gin content to increase the sharpness. The classic lime cordial to use is Rose's, which is readily available in most supermarkets.

INGREDIENTS

2 parts gin
1 part lime cordial

Add the gin and lime cordial to a cocktail shaker filled with cubed ice. Shake the ingredients hard for around 15 seconds and fine strain into a chilled coupe or Martini glass. Garnish with a lime wedge or twist on the rim of the glass.

VESPER

GLASSWARE

Coupe or Martini
glass

GARNISH

Lemon peel

INGREDIENTS

4 parts gin
1 part vodka
½ part dry
vermouth

When one thinks of the Dry Martini, one immediately conjures up images of James Bond uttering the immortal line of "Shaken, not stirred." But the classic Martini is not the only version the British secret agent drank. In the 1953 novel *Casino Royale*, Bond asks a barman to amend the original by adding vodka into the mix. He renames the drink Vesper, christening it after the double agent Vesper Lynd.

Given the wishes of the creator of the Vesper, this is a Martini that must be shaken. Add the ingredients to a cocktail shaker filled with cubed ice and shake hard until condensation appears on the outside of the tin. Fine strain the liquid into a coupe or Martini glass to remove any shards of ice and garnish with a slice of lemon peel.

TUXEDO

GLASSWARE
Coupe or Martini
glass

GARNISH
None

Harry MacElhone is one of the most influential figures in the history of bartending. His legacy lives on with creations such as the Monkey Gland, Between the Sheets, White Lady, and this phenomenal take on the Tuxedo cocktail. Fundamentally, it's a riff between the original Martini and Dry Martini, with sweet and dry ingredients crucial to its success; the additional sugar amplifies the flavor, while the accents of maraschino, absinthe, and orange bitters bring the noise.

INGREDIENTS
1½ parts
Old Tom gin

1½ parts dry
vermouth

3 dashes Angostura
Orange Bitters

1 dash maraschino
liqueur

1 dash absinthe

Add all the ingredients to your cocktail shaker, fill it with cubed ice, and briskly stir for around 15–20 seconds. Strain into a pre-chilled coupe or Martini glass and snap a coin of lemon zest over the drink and then discard.

FRENCH 75

GLASSWARE
Flute

GARNISH
Lemon twist

Created in 1915 at Harry's Bar in Paris, and so named because consuming it was considered reminiscent of being shelled with a 75mm artillery piece, this classic cocktail has aged very well. It can be made with any gin but some of the more modern, citrus-led examples produce a softer, finer beverage. The original calls for Champagne, but it will happily work with your favorite dry sparkling wine.

INGREDIENTS

3 parts gin

1½ parts fresh lemon juice

1½ parts simple syrup (see page 7)

6 parts Champagne

Pour the Champagne into a chilled Champagne flute. Put all the other ingredients into a cocktail shaker with cubed ice and shake. Pour gently over the Champagne, fine straining to remove any ice shards. Garnish with a lemon twist.

PEGU CLUB

Coupe or Martini
glass

Lime wedge

2 parts gin

¾ parts orange
curaçao

¾ parts fresh lime
juice

1 dash Scrappy's
Cardamom Bitters

1 dash Peychaud's
Bitters

The Pegu Club originates from Rangoon's gentleman's establishment of the same name. This twist makes subtle changes to the traditional ingredients by slightly adjusting the ratio and replacing the warm spiced notes of Angostura with the Cardamom Bitters. This introduces a herbal and citrus flavor profile, making every ingredient pop while maintaining the original beverage's style as a drier drink.

Add all the ingredients to a cocktail shaker, fill it with cubed ice, and shake hard for around 10 seconds. Strain into a pre-chilled coupe or Martini glass and garnish with a wedge of fresh lime.

GRAHAM GREENE

GLASSWARE

Coupe or Martini glass

GARNISH

Lemon zest (optional)

This drink was created in the Metropole Hotel in Hanoi for its famous namesake author while he was writing *The Quiet American* in 1951. It breaks Dry Martini convention with a very sweet ingredient, crème de cassis, but the tart character of the blackcurrants pairs nicely with the dry vermouth to balance the drink. Due to the fruity nature of the liqueur, light floral gins work very well in this recipe.

INGREDIENTS

5 parts gin
1 part dry vermouth
1 dash crème de cassis

Stir all the ingredients with cubed ice and strain into a frozen coupe or Martini glass. As with the Martini, you can be flexible with the measurements, but the drink should be pale pink in color, not purple. As crème de cassis will oxidize and go brown, losing the tart berry notes to a caramel sludge taste, it is often sensible to buy miniature bottles of it (and other fruit liqueurs) to ensure less potential wastage. Graham Greene took no garnish, but some lemon zest brings out more freshness and fruit.

19

GIBSON

GLASSWARE

Coupe or Martini
glass

GARNISH

Pickled silverskin
onion

INGREDIENTS

6 parts gin
1 part dry vermouth

The Gibson is the most famous variation on a Martini and differs only in the garnish and the specific ratio of ingredients. Cornichon gherkins, sun-dried tomatoes wrapped in Parma ham, asparagus spears, and a thousand other savory delights make the perfect counterpoint to an ice-cold Gibson.

Stir the gin and vermouth together over cubed ice, aiming to add 1oz (25ml) of water through dilution, and strain into a frozen coupe or Martini glass. Garnish with at least one pickled silverskin onion on a cocktail stick/toothpick. For elegance and taste, try to find small, smooth-skinned pickled onions and limit the amount of pickling liquor transferred to the glass. When in doubt, serve the onions on the side—ideally, the number should be the same as the number of sips taken to consume the drink.

WIBBLE

Created by the UK's most famous bartender, Dick Bradsell, with the tag line: "A Wibble. It might make you wobble but you won't fall over." Sloe gin is technically a liqueur, made by steeping the fruits of the blackthorn (sloes) in gin with equal parts sugar and letting it infuse for many months. The fruit is then removed and the liqueur can be used. The Wibble brings a complex blend of flavors, but is beautifully balanced.

INGREDIENTS

2½ parts gin

2½ parts sloe gin

2½ parts pink
grapefruit juice

1 part simple syrup
(see page 7)

1 part fresh
lemon juice

1 part crème
de mûre

Shake all the ingredients in a cocktail shaker with cubed ice and strain into a chilled coupe or Martini glass. Garnish with a lemon twist.

SOUTHSIDE

GLASSWARE

Coupe or Martini glass

GARNISH

Small mint leaf

Although created in New York, this drink became famed in Chicago, where a version made with crushed ice, similar in style to a Mojito, was drunk during Prohibition by mobsters from the south side of the city. Their competitors from the northern boroughs had to suffer the much less palatable Northside, a mix of gin and ginger ale. The original Southside is served straight up but feel free to try the gangster version. It also forms the basis of the Southside Fizz, served over ice with a spritz of soda water, and the Southside Royale, topped with Champagne. Lighter gins work best here, as the combination of heavy juniper notes and mint can taste a little medicinal.

INGREDIENTS

5 parts gin

2 parts fresh lime juice

2 parts simple syrup (see page 7)

6 mint leaves

Shake all the ingredients in a cocktail shaker with ice cubes and strain into a chilled coupe or Martini glass. Use a fine strainer to remove any small flecks of mint. Garnish with a small mint leaf.

ARMY & NAVY

Coupe or Martini glass

None

2 parts gin

2 dashes Dr. Adam Elmegirab's Boker's Bitters

½ part fresh lemon juice

¼ part orgeat almond syrup

Coin of lemon zest

This drink is credited to Carroll Van Ark, father of American actress Joan Van Ark. The Army & Navy was essentially a simple adaptation of a Gin Sour, replacing the sugar with almond syrup to give it a fragrant, nutty character. The inclusion of bitters is a relatively modern adaptation that makes the ingredients meld together even further, adding to the complexity of the drink.

Add all the ingredients to a cocktail shaker, fill it with cubed ice, and shake hard for around 10 seconds. Strain into a pre-chilled coupe or Martini glass and snap some fresh lemon zest over the drink, then discard the peel.

BEES KNEES

Coupe or Martini
glass

Lemon zest

Honey is a fantastic cocktail ingredient,
but one that is profoundly affected by
temperature—once it begins to chill, it
becomes too thick to incorporate with other
ingredients and sticks to the shaker. To
use it effectively, make it into a syrup. Try
different wild flower honeys to pair with
your chosen gin—orange blossom honey
works well with gin that contains orange as
a botanical, and you can make a delicious
variation of the Bees Knees by adding two
parts fresh orange juice.

2 parts honey syrup
5 parts gin
2 parts fresh
lemon juice

Add all the ingredients to a cocktail shaker
along with a good handful of cubed ice. Shake
hard and strain into a chilled coupe or Martini
glass. Garnish with a slice of lemon zest.

TO MAKE THE HONEY SYRUP, mix
three parts runny honey with
one part hot water and stir until
fully amalgamated and let cool.
This syrup will keep for about
a week in the fridge.

BRAMBLE

Created by Dick Bradsell in London, originally with Bombay Sapphire gin, the Bramble is widely regarded as one of the best cocktails of the dire cocktail decade of the 1980s. It uses crème de mûre, a liqueur made from blackberries, but a good framboise or cassis will make a great variation. Don't feel limited to Bombay Sapphire—although it works well, all but the heaviest gins will make a top Bramble.

INGREDIENTS
5 parts gin
2½ parts fresh lemon juice
1 part simple syrup (see page 7)

Shake the gin, lemon juice, and simple syrup in a cocktail shaker with cubed ice and strain into a large rocks glass, three-quarters full of crushed ice. Top up with more crushed ice and garnish with a lemon slice and a mint sprig. Finally, drizzle in the crème de mûre slowly, so that it "bleeds" through the drink.

ALBION

GLASSWARE

Coupe or Martini
glass

GARNISH

Fresh cherries
(optional)

Cocktail cherries are an abomination—
they can't even be classed as food due to
their harmful ingredients, so can only be
described as a "food decoration." However,
fresh cherries, jams, and liqueurs are
wonderful cocktail ingredients. You can
make this recipe by finely chopping six
seeded cherries and shaking them into the
drink. Try a full-bodied spicy gin to balance
with the rich cherry flavor.

INGREDIENTS

5 parts gin

2 parts fresh
lemon juice

1 part simple syrup
(see page 7)

1 tbsp morello
cherry preserve

½ egg white

Put all the ingredients into a cocktail shaker
and shake, without ice, to incorporate air into
the egg white. Add cubed ice to the shaker and
shake hard, then strain the mix into a chilled
coupe or Martini glass, making sure to include
all the creamy head. This cocktail needs no
garnish but if cherries are in season, it would
be churlish not to add one or two.

BIJOU

Coupe or Martini
glass

GARNISH
Cocktail cherry

Although it has gained a loyal following
in recent years, the Bijou is very much a
drink of the late 1880s. At this time, bars
increasingly sought to create a point of
difference compared to their rivals, and to
cater for increasingly cosmopolitan guests.
So, American bartenders turned to Europe
and the swathe of spirits, amari, vermouth,
liqueurs, and bitters that were available to
strengthen their armory, and they added
new subtleties and complexities to already
established drinks.

INGREDIENTS

1 part Tanqueray
gin

1 part Cocchi
Vermouth di Torino

½ part Green
Chartreuse

1 dash absinthe

1 dash orange
bitters

1 dash Angostura
bitters

Coin of lemon zest

Add all the ingredients to a cocktail shaker, fill
it with cubed ice, and briskly stir for around
15–20 seconds. Strain into a pre-chilled coupe
or Martini glass and garnish with a coin
of lemon zest (snapped over the drink and
discarded) and a cocktail cherry.

SPACE GIN SMASH

GLASSWARE

Rocks glass

GARNISH

Mint sprig,
lemon wedge,
and red grapes

INGREDIENTS

5 parts gin
2 parts apple juice
1½ parts
elderflower cordial

1 part simple syrup
(see page 7)

5 red grapes
5 mint leaves
3 lemon wedges

Created by master bartender Pete Kendall at Trailer Happiness in London, the Space Gin Smash is a consistent best-seller on every menu where it has appeared. The crowd-pleasing ingredients are in perfect balance and suitable for any occasion, which makes it stunningly easy to have not just one or two Smashes, but one or two too many. It really is a true modern classic. Any gin will work here, from Hendrick's to Tanqueray, so experiment at will.

There are a couple of ways to make this drink. The original recipe calls for the grapes and the lemon wedges to be muddled first, with the other ingredients then added and swizzled with crushed ice. This tastes delicious but can look a bit "rustic."

For a prettier drink, muddle all the ingredients in the shaker, and shake and strain over cubed ice. Don't be tempted to substitute the lemon wedges for lemon juice, though—the oils extracted during muddling are a vital ingredient. Garnish with a mint sprig, lemon wedge, and a grape or two.

CLOVER CLUB

GLASSWARE
Coupe or Martini
glass

GARNISH
None

INGREDIENTS
1½ parts
raspberry syrup

4½ parts gin

1½ parts dry
vermouth

2 parts fresh
lemon juice

½ egg white

As with many classic cocktails, there are arguments over the Clover Club's creation and its recipe—some omit the dry vermouth entirely while others call for a dash of sweet vermouth in addition or instead. Certainly, the drink has been popular since the 1930s and is still universally well received today.

Shake all the ingredients in a cocktail shaker without ice to emulsify the egg white. Add cubed ice and shake until the liquid is cooled. Strain into a chilled coupe or Martini glass.

TO MAKE RASPBERRY SYRUP, push ripe raspberries through a fine strainer and mix the resultant juice with an equal weight of superfine (caster) sugar. Alternatively, add simple syrup (see page 7) and 5 raspberries to the shaker—remembering to fine strain at the end to remove any seeds.

ROYAL TRIBUTE

GLASSWARE
Coupe or Martini glass

GARNISH
Orange twist

INGREDIENTS
⅛ part Green Chartreuse

⅛ part maraschino liqueur

1 part Martini Rosso vermouth

1 part Bombay Sapphire gin

¼ part gomme syrup

Champagne, ice cold

This cocktail was invented in 2011 by Daniel Baernreuther at the Savoy to celebrate the marriage of Prince William and Kate Middleton. It was served at the hotel's American Bar in the run up to the wedding and captured the mood perfectly.

Pre-chill a coupe or Martini glass. Pour all the ingredients, except the Champagne, over ice in a mixing jug. Stir. Strain into the glass. Top up with the Champagne and garnish with the orange twist.

HEDGEROW SLING

Highball

Lemon slice,
blackberries,
and raspberry

Perhaps the tastiest Collins recipe ever, the
Hedgerow Sling has it all: complexity of
flavor but still refreshing, a suitable size that
should last for a while, and very pretty to
boot. The drink relies on the best ingredients
and stands tall as is, but if you are able to get
hold of good-quality ripe fall fruits, such as
raspberries, blackberries, or redcurrants, add
a few into the shaker for that extra dimension.
Try with a London dry gin like Beefeater.

2½ parts gin
2½ parts sloe gin
2 parts fresh
lemon juice
1 part simple syrup
(see page 7)
5 parts soda water
1½ parts crème
de mûre

Shake all the ingredients in a cocktail shaker,
except for the soda water and crème de mûre,
and strain over cubed ice into a sling glass.
Add a little crushed ice and top with soda
water. As a final touch, slowly drizzle the
crème de mûre over the top, so that it "bleeds"
down through the drink. Garnish with a
lemon slice and a berry or two.

31

SINGAPORE SLING

GLASSWARE
Highball

GARNISH
Lemon zest curl and
a cocktail cherry

INGREDIENTS
1 part gin

1 part cherry
brandy

1 barspoon
Benedictine

1 part fresh
lemon juice

1 small dash
Angostura bitters

Soda water,
to top up

Created at the Long Bar at the Raffles hotel in Singapore, when this drink is made correctly, and without using one of the cheap pre-mixes that are so prevalent today, it is the peak of sophistication! The original Singapore Sling recipe has long been a subject of hot debate; this is one of the best.

Put all the ingredients in a small pitcher/jug filled with ice and stir gently to mix. Top up with soda water. Serve in a tall, ice-filled glass, garnished with a lemon zest curl and a cocktail cherry.

GIN SLING

Here is a drink so old—well over 200 years—that it predates the cocktail. The slings took 19th-century America by storm, and it's a testament to its charm that it is still a joy to drink today. This version updates the traditional serve by adding a slug of cherry brandy, which makes slinging one back even more of a treat.

GLASSWARE

Wine glass or highball

GARNISH

Lemon wedge

INGREDIENTS

2 parts fresh lemon juice

1 part simple syrup

3 parts gin

1¼ parts cherry brandy

Soda water, to top up

Put all the ingredients, except the soda water, into a shaker, with ice. Shake vigorously and strain into a pre-chilled glass. Top up with soda water.

NEGRONI

The Negroni takes its name from Count Camillo Negroni, an habitué of the Casoni bar in Florence, just after World War I. After a bad day, the Count asked the bartender for his favored Americano cocktail, but "with a bit more kick." The bartender added a slug of gin, the Count was impressed, and very soon other patrons would call for Negroni's drink. This cocktail is all about balance—the standard recipe calls for equal parts of all the ingredients, but don't be afraid to adjust them for personal preference. If you find Campari too bitter, reduce the amount used, and feel free to experiment with different styles of gin and sweet vermouth.

INGREDIENTS
2½ parts gin
2½ parts Campari
2½ parts sweet
vermouth

Stir all the ingredients with cubed ice in a large rocks glass, and garnish with a slice of orange.

3

VERMOUTH

GIN

CAMPARI

Italian!

n

SNOW ANGEL

Coupe or Martini glass

Grated lemon zest and silver spoon

4 parts gin
1 part Cointreau
2 parts fresh lemon juice
1 part simple syrup (see page 7)
½ egg white
1 scoop lemon sorbet

This drink has its roots in the White Lady (see page 59), a classic mix of gin and Cointreau with fresh lemon. The addition of the lemon sorbet brings an extra texture and a bit of fun, making this a great party drink. It also works very well as a palate cleanser at a dinner party—simply halve the quantities and serve in smaller glasses.

Put all the ingredients, apart from the sorbet, into the cocktail shaker and shake hard, without ice, to start to emulsify the egg white. Fill the shaker with cubed ice and shake again. Strain into a chilled coupe or Martini glass and place a scoop of sorbet in the center of the glass. Garnish with grated lemon zest and a spoon.

LONDON CALLING

GLASSWARE
Coupe or Martini
glass

GARNISH
Grapefruit zest

INGREDIENTS
1½ parts
Beefeater gin

½ part fino sherry

3 dashes orange
bitters

½ part fresh
lemon juice

½ part simple syrup
(see page 7)

Created in 2002 by Chris Jepson, then of London's Milk & Honey, the London Calling bridges the gap between classical and modern cocktail movements. The drink is perfectly balanced, with the fruit and nut notes of the sherry complementing the orange and spice notes offered up by the gin.

Add all the ingredients to a cocktail shaker, fill it with cubed ice, and shake hard for around 10 seconds. Strain into a pre-chilled coupe or Martini glass and garnish with a coin of fresh grapefruit zest, snapped over and then dropped into the drink.

GIN AND TONIC

GLASSWARE
Highball

GARNISH
Lemon or lime
wedge

INGREDIENTS
2oz (50ml) gin
Tonic water,
to top up

Observe these rules to elevate a humble
G&T into something outstanding:

★ The drink should be served ice cold, so keep
the tonic in the fridge and the ice in the
freezer until the last moment.

★ Pick your garnish according to the character
of the gin. Some gins work with cucumber,
grapefruit, or even strawberries, but
generally you can't go wrong with citrus—
either bold lime or gentler lemon.

★ Don't scrimp on the gin, you need at least
2oz (50ml) to be able to taste the alcohol,
with the botanicals in the spirit working
their magic alongside those in the tonic.

★ Tonic makes up most of the glass so try
different brands until you find a perfect
match. Use single-serve bottles or cans,
otherwise the tonic will go flat.

★ Add a flavored liqueur. A dash of sloe gin or
elderflower liqueur is an excellent choice.

Start by preparing your chosen garnish, then
fill a glass with cubed ice and pour over the
gin. Take the tonic out of the fridge and pour
into the glass, filling it to around ½in/1cm
below the rim. Once the bubbles have settled,
give everything a quick stir. Add the garnish but
don't squeeze; this can overpower the drink.

RED SNAPPER

GLASSWARE
Highball

GARNISH
Celery stick

Perhaps less well-known than its famous sibling, the Bloody Mary, the Red Snapper switches up vodka for gin, adding an extra botanical element to the flavor profile which makes for a more well-rounded drink. The recipe is open to experimentation—up the amount of Tabasco if you like things spicy, while an extra dash or two of Worcestershire sauce can enhance the savory, umami content of this hair of the dog cocktail. Celery salt is also a welcome addition, but not essential if you don't have any in your spice rack.

INGREDIENTS
2 parts gin
4 parts tomato juice
4 dashes Tabasco
Pinch of celery salt (optional)
½ part fresh lemon juice
1 pinch of freshly ground black pepper
4 dashes Worcestershire sauce

Fill a cocktail shaker with cubed ice and add all the ingredients. Give the tin a shake and strain into a highball glass filled with cubed ice. Garnish with a large celery stick, stood upright in the glass.

TOM COLLINS

GLASSWARE
Highball

GARNISH
Lemon slice
and cherry

The Tom Collins—gin and sparkling lemonade—was probably inadvertently "invented" about five minutes after Jacob Schweppe invented soda water in 1783. Certainly, the Tom Collins was popular worldwide by the 1850s. The basic recipe is delicious, allowing the character of different gins to be compared. It is a great test-drive for a new gin—if a brand makes a good Tom Collins, then it is likely to work in a great many other cocktails.

INGREDIENTS
6 parts gin
2½ parts fresh
lemon juice
3 parts simple syrup
(see page 7)
6 parts soda water

Lightly shake the gin, lemon juice, and syrup, together with any extra desired ingredients (see opposite) in a cocktail shaker, and strain over cubed ice into a tall highball glass. Top with soda water. Garnish with a lemon slice and a good-quality conserved cherry or other appropriate fruit.

ELDERFLOWER COLLINS

GLASSWARE
Highball

GARNISH
Lemon slice and mint sprig

INGREDIENTS
6 parts gin

2½ parts fresh lemon juice

2 parts elderflower cordial

6 parts soda water

Fruits and purées, liqueurs, and other citrus fruits can all be incorporated into the basic Collins recipe, taking advantage of any local produce or bottles you might have in your cocktail cabinet. In this case, the simple syrup is replaced by elderflower cordial and its floral notes latch onto the botanicals present in the gin to give a refreshing cocktail that's dangerously drinkable.

Follow the method for the Tom Collins (opposite), but replace the simple syrup with the elderflower cordial. Top up the highball glass with soda water and garnish with a slice of lemon and a sprig of mint.

CROQUET CLUB COBBLER

Wine glass or highball

1 blueberry,
1 blackberry,
1 raspberry, and
1 slice cucumber

3 chunks fresh
pineapple (approx
1in./2.5cm cubes)

2 bar spoons
superfine (caster)
sugar

1½ parts fresh
lemon juice

⅔ part fino sherry

1 part elderflower
liqueur

3 parts
Hendrick's gin

This more complex version of a traditional Cobbler benefits from the addition of delicious St Germain elderflower liqueur, a popular drinks modifier. So popular in fact that it's developed the nickname "bartender's ketchup."

Pre-chill a glass. Muddle the pineapple, sugar, and lemon juice at the bottom of a shaker. Add the rest of the ingredients and top up with ice. Shake vigorously. Strain into the chilled glass, with ice, and garnish with the fruit and cucumber slice.

VELVET SLEDGEHAMMER

GLASSWARE
Tankard

GARNISH
Lemon slice, apple slice, or apple fan

INGREDIENTS
4 parts gin
2 parts passionfruit syrup
1½ parts fresh lemon juice
12 parts medium-dry hard apple cider, ideally at least 6% ABV

Gin and passionfruit is a marriage made in heaven. In fact, it's so good that it's surprising no one has used it as a botanical. You can make passionfruit syrup at home but it is much easier to buy a commercial brand for consistency—Monin is a good bet. A strong, juniper-led gin works best, integrating with the fragrant passionfruit and dry apple notes from the cider.

Shake the gin, passionfruit syrup, and lemon juice in a cocktail shaker, then strain the mix over cubed ice into a tankard or handled beer glass. Top with the hard cider. Garnish with a lemon slice and apple slice or fan. This drink works really well as a sharing punch, just multiply the ingredients and serve in a pitcher or punch bowl.

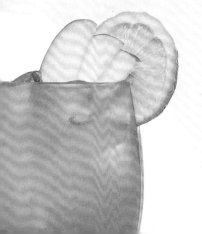

GIN LANE

GLASSWARE
Highball

GARNISH
Mint sprig and a
marinated cherry

Bombay Sapphire has always seemed a very exotic name for a gin, reminiscent of the British Raj and magnificent jewels. The particular sapphire referred to here is the 182-carat "Star of Bombay" at the Smithsonian Institution. It's quite a rock— and Gin Lane is quite a cocktail. To top off the treat, the garnish includes a marinated cherry, prepared by steeping the fruit with cherry liqueur, Angostura bitters, and simple syrup.

INGREDIENTS
4 parts Bombay
Sapphire gin

1 part apricot
liqueur

1 part Grand
Marnier

2½ parts fresh
lemon juice

2 parts orgeat
almond syrup

Ginger ale,
to top up

Combine the ingredients in a shaker; fill up with ice. Shake; then strain into a highball glass. Top up with ginger ale. Fill up with ice cubes and garnish with the mint and a cherry.

ENGLISH MOJITO

GLASSWARE
Highball

GARNISH
Large mint sprig

INGREDIENTS
10 mint leaves
5 parts gin
1½ parts
elderflower cordial
1 part simple syrup
(see page 7)
2½ parts fresh
lemon juice

Although this recipe is obviously based on a rum drink, it is arguable that the marriage of gin and mint is even better. Elderflower is a quintessentially English ingredient, which also works very nicely with gin, and the cordial is widely available and very versatile. Most gins will work well in this recipe, but if you have either Miller's or Hendrick's gin, please try it, as the cucumber notes go really well together.

Gently bruise and tear the mint leaves and place in a highball glass, then add the other ingredients and a scoop of crushed ice. Vigorously swizzle or churn the mixture to incorporate the mint and dilute slightly. Top up with more crushed ice to form a crown of ice proud of the drink—this improves the presentation and also reduces the speed of further dilution by acting as an ice duvet. Garnish with a large mint sprig right underneath the straw.

RASPBERRY RICKEY

GLASSWARE
Highball

GARNISH
Lime wedge and
a raspberry

In the late nineteenth century, Rickeys were all the rage, with a base liquor being softened up by a healthy dose of soda water and a wedge of lime. For the Washington bartenders that created the drink—named after Colonel Joe Rickey—bourbon was the spirit of choice, before others began experimenting with gin as an alternative. Sadly, the Rickey's decline in popularity is inversely proportional to the rise of the G&T as the gin drink of the masses. However, as is the case with many long-forgotten cocktails, drink historians have revived the venerable Rickey and tinkered with it to invent interesting alternatives like this version.

INGREDIENTS
5 raspberries
½ lime, cut into
wedges
3 parts gin
1 dash Chambord
Soda water, to top up

Place the raspberries in a cocktail shaker and add the lime juice, gin, and Chambord. Muddle the ingredients together and fine strain the liquid into a highball glass. Fill the glass with cracked ice and top up with the soda water. To finish, garnish with a wedge of lime and a raspberry.

10CC

Originally created with Tanqueray 10, as referenced by the name, this drink pairs the warming spice of chamomile with the crisp freshness of cucumber. Tanqueray 10 uses fresh citrus peels in its recipe, alongside chamomile as a botanical, making it the perfect ingredient for this recipe. A spray of grapefruit zest will complete the picture. Although designed with a specific spirit in mind, this cocktail works well with any gin with a healthy ABV.

GARNISH

3 cucumber slices

INGREDIENTS

3 cucumber slices
5 parts gin
2½ parts
chamomile syrup
2 parts fresh
lemon juice
6 parts soda water

Muddle the cucumber in a cocktail shaker, add all the other ingredients, except for the soda water, and shake. Strain over cubed ice in a highball glass and top with the soda water. Garnish with cucumber slices.

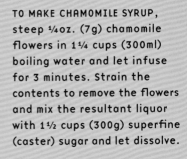

TO MAKE CHAMOMILE SYRUP, steep ¼oz. (7g) chamomile flowers in 1¼ cups (300ml) boiling water and let infuse for 3 minutes. Strain the contents to remove the flowers and mix the resultant liquor with 1½ cups (300g) superfine (caster) sugar and let dissolve.

GIN SOUR

Coupe or Martini glass

Lemon peel

2 parts gin

1 part fresh lemon juice

1 part simple syrup (see page 7)

1 egg white

1 dash Angostura bitters

This is a slightly twisted version of the traditional Gin Sour recipe, as it involves using egg white to add a smooth mouthfeel to counterbalance the signature sharpness of the drink. Feel free to omit the egg if desired, but if you choose to include it you will be rewarded with an easy drinking, lightly textured cocktail.

Add the ingredients except the bitters to a cocktail shaker without ice and shake hard for at least 30 seconds to allow the egg white to emulsify. Next, add cubed ice to the tin and shake for 10 seconds to chill the drink. Fine strain into a chilled coupe or Martini glass and allow to settle, you should see a thick foam form at the top of the glass. To finish, add a dash or two of Angostura bitters.

RASPARI

Coupe or Martini
glass

GARNISH
Raspberry

Created by a young bartender Vincenzo Errico to showcase one of his favorite ingredients, this cocktail is a great way to start appreciating beverage bitters like Campari. The fresh raspberries and raspberry liqueur dial back the bitterness and make a very approachable but complex drink. This drink works best with fresh raspberries in season. If unavailable, frozen raspberries or purée make a good substitute and are normally less expensive too.

INGREDIENTS

3 parts gin
1 part Campari
2 parts fresh
lemon juice
5 raspberries
1 part Chambord
1 part simple syrup
(see page 7)

Put all the ingredients in the cocktail shaker—there is no need to muddle the raspberries first, as they are soft enough to break up completely during shaking—with some cubed ice and shake hard. Fine strain the contents into a chilled coupe or Martini glass to remove any seeds. Garnish with a single raspberry floating in the center of the glass.

AVIATION

Harking back to the age of those magnificent men and their flying machines, the Aviation is credited to Hugo Ensslin, the head bartender at New York's celebrated Hotel Wallick, who featured the drink in his 1916 book *Recipes for Mixed Drinks*. The cocktail disappeared for a while due to the fact that crème de violette was not readily available. Thankfully that's changed and Aviations have become a common feature on menus at many quality drinking establishments.

GLASSWARE

Coupe or Martini glass

GARNISH

Lemon twist

INGREDIENTS

3 parts gin

1 part fresh lemon juice

1 part maraschino liqueur

1 dash crème de violette

Put all the ingredients into a cocktail shaker along with some cubed ice. Give the ingredients a hard shake for around 15–20 seconds, until the contents are chilled and the ice diluted to take the edge off the alcohol. Fine strain carefully into a chilled coupe or Martini glass to remove any particles of ice and lemon, then garnish with a lemon twist.

CASINO

As mentioned opposite for the Aviation, crème de violette isn't the easiest ingredient to get hold of and it still takes a bit of searching to uncover a bottle. If you can't track down the violet liqueur, you can still make the drink without it and the resulting Casino cocktail is the perfect mix of sweet and citrus. The maraschino provides a pleasing sugary hit that is counterbalanced by the citrus zing of the lemon juice and orange bitters.

Take your cocktail shaker, add the ingredients, and fill with cubed ice. Give the tin a good shake to cool everything down before straining into a chilled coupe or Martini glass. Take your orange peel and give it a twist or alternatively spear your cocktail cherry onto a cocktail stick/toothpick and add to the glass.

CORPSE REVIVER NO. 2

Here's an adaptation of another Harry Craddock classic, which is designed to shake off the shackles of a particularly menacing hangover and have you back on your feet after just a few sips. The original recipe calls for Kina Lillet, which is no longer available, but any brand of dry vermouth will be a perfectly serviceable replacement.

INGREDIENTS
1 part gin
1 part orange liqueur
1 part fresh lemon juice
1 part dry vermouth
1 dash absinthe

Before you start, decide how you want to include the absinthe. You can either add it to the mix with the other ingredients, or swirl the spirit in the coupe or Martini glass and discard before you start on the rest of the drink. Once you've made your decision, add all the ingredients into a cocktail shaker filled with cubed ice and shake hard for around 20 seconds. Strain the liquid into the chilled (possibly absinthe-rinsed) glass and garnish with the lemon peel, squeezing it first to release some of the citrus oils.

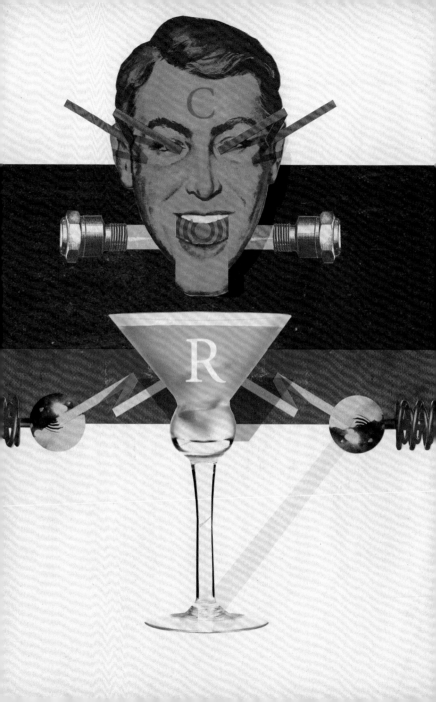

GIN PAHIT

Coupe or Martini glass

Coin of fresh lemon zest

Pickled onions, to serve (optional)

Gin Pahit, or "bitter gin" in Malay, is largely responsible for the success of Angostura Bitters. While serving for Venezuelan leader Simón Bolívar in the port of Angostura, Dr. Johann Gottlieb Benjamin Siegert began marketing his bitters to sailors as a cure for seasickness. Quickly gaining in popularity with the Royal Navy, sailors began adding dashes of the new elixir to gin, and so the Pink Gin was born. It would later be the colonies in British Malaya who would up the ratio of bitters for the Pahit, as a way to adjust stomachs to the new climate.

3 parts Plymouth gin

1 part Angostura bitters

¹/₃ part simple syrup (see page 7)

Add all the ingredients to a cocktail shaker, fill it with cubed ice, and briskly stir for around 15–20 seconds. Strain into a chilled coupe or Martini glass and garnish with lemon zest. Optionally, serve onions pickled in chili vinegar as a side.

GARRICK
GIN PUNCH

GLASSWARE

Coupe or Martini
glass

GARNISH

Lemon zest

INGREDIENTS

2 parts London
dry gin

1 part fresh
lemon juice

½ part maraschino
liqueur

1 dash simple syrup
(see page 7)

2 dashes Angostura
bitters

If the dryness of a good London gin is your thing then this is your cocktail. A superb choice for an aperitif, this cocktail will cut through the fug of your day and prepare your palate for whatever the evening holds. Shake it until it's as cold as can be and serve in a chilled glass.

Add all the ingredients to a cocktail shaker filled with ice and shake together until the outside of the shaker starts to frost. Strain into a frosted coupe or Martini glass and serve garnished with a thin piece of lemon zest.

PENDENNIS CLUB COCKTAIL

GLASSWARE
Coupe or Martini glass

GARNISH
Cocktail cherry

First established in Louisville, Kentucky, in 1881, the Pendennis Club has earned global renown in the world of cocktails for the venue's claim to be the birthplace of the Old Fashioned. Strangely, it was only in recent years that you could order the Pendennis Club Cocktail at the club following the introduction of a drinks menu showcasing the various cocktails served at the bar over the last century. The drink itself is primarily tart with a flavor not too dissimilar to grapefruit, but also subtly sweet with a stoned fruit flavor throughout and a spicy, bracing finish from the bitters. A truly exceptional cocktail that deserves more acclaim.

INGREDIENTS
2 parts gin
1 part apricot brandy
3/4 part fresh lime juice
2 dashes Peychaud's Bitters

Add all the ingredients to a cocktail shaker, fill with cubed ice, and shake hard for 10 seconds. Strain into a pre-chilled coupe or Martini glass and garnish with a cocktail cherry.

TRICOLORE

Coupe or Martini glass

Cocktail cherry and lime twist

2 parts London dry gin

½ part limoncello

¾ part fino sherry

½ part simple syrup (see page 7), infused for several hours with a vanilla bean/pod

1 part fresh lemon juice

Created by Agostino Perrone, head bartender at London's Connaught Bar, this drink pays homage to three places important in his life: gin from London, sherry from Spain, and limoncello from his home country, Italy. The colors also represent the Italian tricolore flag.

Shake all the ingredients over ice and double-strain into a pre-chilled coupe or Martini glass. (If you have used ice to chill the glass, discard it.) Garnish with the cherry and lime twist.

58

WHITE LADY

Coupe or Martini
glass

None

Some things are best left unadorned. The White Lady cocktail is undoubtedly one such example, it is a drink so glamorous that no garnish is needed to attract attention. Here the glass is thoroughly chilled before pouring into it the light, frothy, and deliciously citrussy mix.

1 part fresh
lemon juice

1 part Cointreau

2 parts gin

½ white of 1 egg

Pre-chill a coupe or Martini glass with ice. Pour all the ingredients into a shaker and fill with ice. Shake vigorously. Discard the ice in the glass. Strain the mixture into the glass.

RAMOS FIZZ

One of the few classic cocktails with a history beyond dispute, the Ramos Fizz was created in 1888 by Henry C. Ramos in New Orleans and originally called the New Orleans Fizz. Ramos kept the recipe a secret and feared his drink would die with the advent of Prohibition, but following his death in 1928, Ramos' brother posthumously released the recipe in his honor.

INGREDIENTS

5 parts gin

1 part fresh lemon juice

1 part fresh lime juice

2 parts simple syrup (see page 7)

2 parts single cream

1 egg white

Orange flower water (add a drop at a time, the flavor is intense)

Soda water, to top up

Shake all the ingredients, except the soda water, hard in a shaker for at least a few minutes (the original recipe calls for 12!). Add some ice cubes and shake briefly to chill. Strain into a wine glass or highball with ice. Top up with the soda water.

SLOE GIN FIZZ

In Great Britain, there's a tradition of making your own sloe gin using fruit foraged on crisp autumnal walks. The liqueur is now gaining a fan base outside of its traditional home, with producers popping up in the US and beyond. You may need to play around with the balance of flavors in this cocktail, as different brands of sloe gin have varying degrees of sweetness.

INGREDIENTS

2½ parts sloe gin

1 part fresh lemon juice

1 dash simple syrup (see page 7)

Soda water, to top up

Add all the ingredients, except the soda, to a shaker filled with ice. Shake sharply and strain into a highball glass filled with ice. Top with soda water and garnish with a lemon slice.

GREEN PARK

Rocks glass

Fresh basil sprig

INGREDIENTS

6 leaves fresh basil

3 drops celery bitters

1 part fresh lemon juice

½ part simple syrup (see page 7)

1½ parts Old Tom gin

½ egg white

Thanks to the use of fresh basil and celery bitters, the vegetal notes of the Green Park are beguiling, bringing a freshness to the drink that's reminiscent of a crisp, clear spring morning. This is complemented by a superb silkiness, thanks to the egg white, but an important part of confecting this delicacy is the double-straining.

Fill a glass with crushed ice and set aside to chill. Put all the ingredients in a shaker and top up with ice. Shake. Discard the ice from the glass. Double-strain the mixture into the glass and garnish with the basil sprig.

INDEX

RECIPE CREDITS

Michael Butt: pages 8, 17, 19–22, 24–6, 28–9, 31, 34, 36, 40, 43, 45, 47, 49
Adam Elmegirab: pages 10, 16, 18, 23, 27, 37, 54, 56
Ben Reed: pages 11, 14–15, 32, 39, 41, 46, 55, 61
William Yeoward: pages 12, 30, 33, 42, 44, 58–60, 62
Dog 'n' Bone: 38, 48, 50–2

PICTURE CREDITS

Terry Benson: pages 10, 16, 18, 23, 27, 37, 54, 56
Addie Chinn: 34
Gavin Kingcome: pages 12, 30, 33, 42, 44, 58–60, 62–3
William Lingwood: pages 32, 55, 61
Alex Luck: page 7
Martin Norris: pages 14,–15, 17, 19–22, 24–6, 28–9, 31, 38–41, 43, 45–51